How a Horse Grew Hoarse on the Site Where He Sighted a Bare Bear

pictures by Lorna Tomei

How a Horse Grew Hoarse on the Site Where He Sighted a Bare Bear

A TALE OF HOMONYMS by

Emily Hanlon

Delacorte Press
New York

For my father, for helping me smooth out the wrinkles. —E. H.

For Gordon, Ethan and Terrence —L. T.

Text Copyright © 1976 by Emily J. Tarasov

Illustrations Copyright © 1976 by Lorna Tomei

All rights reserved. No part of this book may be reproduced in any form or by any means without the prior written permission of the Publisher, excepting brief quotes used in connection with reviews written specifically for inclusion in a magazine or newspaper.

Manufactured in the United States of America

First printing

Library of Congress Cataloging in Publication Data

Hanlon, Emily.
 How a horse grew hoarse on the site where he sighted a bare bear.

 SUMMARY: Using more than forty pairs of homonyms, relates in verse how the bear, deer, horse, bee, hare, gnu, ewe, witch, tern, and "me" set sail to see the sea.
 [1. Nonsense verses. 2. English language — Homonyms — Poetry] I. Tomei, Lorna. II. Title.
PZ8.3.H1944Ho   811'.5'4   75-26682
ISBN 0-440-03832-4
ISBN 0-440-03833-2 lib. bdg.

The sky was blue.
The sun was bright.
The weather was just grand.
We got in a boat to see the sea:
the bear, the deer, the horse, the bee,
the hare, the gnu, the ewe,
the witch, the tern and me.
We came all dressed in our party best.
We came, you see, for tea.

The boat set sail with the gnu at the wheel.
"How dandy you look!" said the deer with a squeal.
"Why, thank you," said the gnu, bowing quite low,
and he tangled his tie in his great big toe.
"Oh, dear!" cried the gnu. "Please help me to ease,
the pain in my toe in this terrible squeeze!"
But the silly deer, she just loved to tease,
so she laughed and ignored the gnu's sad pleas.

"Please, somebody help me! I'm all in a knot!"
moaned the gnu who by now was nervous and hot.
"Did someone say 'knot'?" snapped the quarrelsome hare.
"Not me," baaed the ewe in a wail of despair.
"So it's you—you ewe!" cried the hare with a shriek.
"Who, me?" asked the ewe who was meeker than meek.
"Yes, you, silly ewe. You're a terrible sight!
With your hair all in knots—you're an absolute fright!"

So it's you-you ewe!

"There's not a knot in her hair," the horse neighed with pride.
"The hair on the ewe is soft, curled and tied.
But look at the bear! Is he dressed for tea?
He's naked as naked as naked can be!"

"Oh, dear, oh, dear," cried the deer with a titter.
"Oh, dear, dear, dear," and her tone was bitter.
Her face grew red and she started to plead,
"A bear with no clothes is a bare bear, indeed!
I will close my eyes so as not to see."
The bear just wondered what the fuss could be.

Then the tern, who'd said not a word till now,
looked down from her perch on the sail near the bow.
And seeing the disorderly scene below,
said, "I think it's time for me to go.
There's too much noise for me to stay."
So the tern turned around and flew away.
The others didn't hear this gentle, wise bird,
for below on the deck all the noise was absurd!

While the bee was buzzing and buzzing "I'll be,"
the happy old horse was neighing with glee,
for he really enjoyed the scene he had made.
So he neighed till his voice began to fade.
And then he started to groan in pain
for he'd grown so hoarse it seemed in vain
to believe that he'd ever talk again.

When I thought the noise would never cease,
the ugly, old witch called out for "Peace!"
"Take a piece of advice from me today.
Stop your bickering! Stop I say!"
"Which witch are you?" then asked the hare.
And the witch looked at him with a deadly glare.
And shrieked, "Your behavior is too much to bear!"

And then with a great and terrible cry,
she snapped her fingers into the sky.
From the sky came a book with pages red.
She opened the book and from it she read:

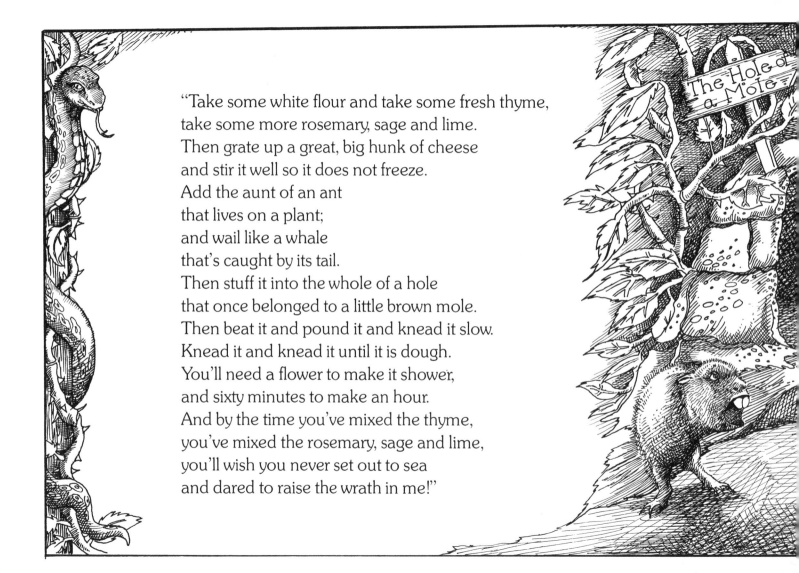

"Take some white flour and take some fresh thyme,
take some more rosemary, sage and lime.
Then grate up a great, big hunk of cheese
and stir it well so it does not freeze.
Add the aunt of an ant
that lives on a plant;
and wail like a whale
that's caught by its tail.
Then stuff it into the whole of a hole
that once belonged to a little brown mole.
Then beat it and pound it and knead it slow.
Knead it and knead it until it is dough.
You'll need a flower to make it shower,
and sixty minutes to make an hour.
And by the time you've mixed the thyme,
you've mixed the rosemary, sage and lime,
you'll wish you never set out to sea
and dared to raise the wrath in me!"

The Hole a Mole

And as she spoke, her words came true.
Our sky lost all of its lovely blue.
Hard blew the wind and black grew the sky.
And thunder and lightning roared on high.

It seemed like a seam of heaven had burst.
We huddled together and feared for the worst.
In the sky we saw a creature soar by
with bolts of lightning in each eye.
Behind him we heard other creatures roar.
We heard that herd and our ears grew sore.

They stormed on by, the rain poured down.
The witch looked up with a terrible frown.
Her face was lit with a strange new light,
and she waved her arms with all her might.
"He's the Prince of the Sky and the Son of the Sun!
He's the King of the Rain, the Powerful One!
And with him come his mighty men,
the Knights of the Night, who number ten.
Rain will reign over the ocean as King.
And you foolish creatures will feel his sting!
Look about you! Can't you see?
It twirls and rages at you and me!"

And as she spoke she waved her cape
and down from the sky came her escape.
A stairway of silver and gold, so fair,
took her away in the cold, dark air.

"Oh, dear!" cried the deer and she grew quite pale.
"Don't cry," warned the horse with a swish of his tail.
"No time for a tale of woe," he frowned.
"Bail with that pail or we'll all be drowned!"
The deer was so frightened she did not hear,
And cried out, "Of course! The end is near!"

"The point here," said the bear to the horse,
"is whether the boat can stay on course.
Or whether the boat can weather the weather.
And whether we all can make it together.
I've seen a scene like this before.
And I know it's peace we need — not war!"

For four long days our boat was tossed
until we were sure that we were lost.
The hare, who was always ready to fight,
shivered with fear and prayed for light.
And the gentle ewe just held him tight
and sang him a hymn to ease his fright.

The gnu was still in a terrible state;
with his toe in his tie, we feared for his fate.
When all of a sudden that silly deer
came to her senses and said, "Do not fear."
The boat stopped tossing for a minute or two,
she bit open the knot and his toe slipped through.

And then the gnu went back to the wheel;
an expert sailor, he steadied the keel.
"Don't mourn," he said as he took command.
"I promise by morn you'll all see land."

When morning came, to our delight,
his words came true; land was in sight.
The sea was calm. The sky was bright.
And home we sailed — with not one fight.

A list of homonyms used:

ant, aunt
bare, bear
be, bee
blue, blew
clothes, close
course, coarse
deer, dear
ewe, you
flour, flower
four, for
grate, great
groan, grown
hare, hair
herd, heard

here, hear   scene, seen

him, hymn   see, sea

horse, hoarse   seem, seam

hour, our   sight, site

I, *eye*   soar, sore

knead, need   son, sun

knight, night   tail, tale

knot, not   thyme, time

morn, mourn   to, too

pale, pail   turn, tern

peace, piece   wail, whale

please, pleas   whether, weather

rain, reign   which, witch

red, read   whole, hole

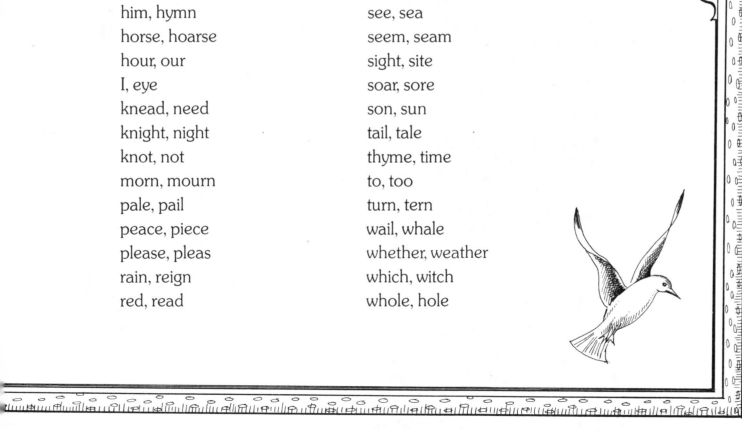

ABOUT THE AUTHOR

EMILY HANLON was born in New York City and grew up in Westchester County, New York, where she now lives with her family. She attended the Dalton High School and Barnard College. She married Ned Tarasov while still in college. When her two children, Nicky and Natasha, started school, Emily Hanlon began teaching retarded adults. When she realized that she really wanted to write, she stopped teaching to devote full time to children's books. This is her second book; her first book, *What If a Lion Eats Me and I Fall into a Hippopotamus' Mud Hole?*, with pictures by Leigh Grant, was recently published by Delacorte Press.

ABOUT THE ARTIST

LORNA TOMEI was born and grew up in Queens, New York. She studied at the Art Students League, The School of Visual Arts and New York University, all in Manhattan. She has done illustrations for several educational media, including filmstrips, and has designed toys. This is the second picture book she has illustrated. Ms. Tomei lives in Queens, New York, with her husband, also an artist, and their two children.

ABOUT THE BOOK

The illustrations were drawn on Strathmore drawing paper. A Rapidograph pen was used with a variety of pen nibs including three zero and four zero. A fine crow quill pen was also used to add different textures to some of the drawings. The text of the book has been set in Souvenir light with Souvenir medium for display by The Composing Room, Inc.

It was designed by Lynn Braswell.